NEW ADVENTURES IN
ORIGAMI

New Adventures in Origami

The Art of Paper-Folding

Robert Harbin

BARNES & NOBLE BOOKS
A DIVISION OF HARPER & ROW, PUBLISHERS
New York, Cambridge, Philadelphia
San Francisco, London, Mexico City
São Paulo, Sydney

To the Memory of
Ligia Montoya of Argentina

CONTENTS

PREFACE

Origami in paperback has, thanks to you, dear enthusiasts, been an unqualified success and is in fact a bestseller.

The appeal of Origami as an intellectual pastime for young and old is now so great that I have done my best to provide, for experts and beginners alike, a further collection of exciting folds in the shape of *New Adventures in Origami*.

Because I am an Origami addict myself I have tried to give you as wide a selection as possible, generously provided by folders from all parts of the world. May I add that the selection would have been even wider had it not been for a Post Office strike which happened at the time of writing.

If you are paper-folding for the first time you will be well advised to get hold of a copy of *Origami* (Funk & Wagnalls), because although this book is complete within itself the two books are even more so.

As Origami gains popularity as an art form, certain names are becoming important among the faithful. America is producing some outstanding material and a long list of creative folders, so I hope I will be forgiven if I only mention the two giants of Origami, Neal Elias and Frederick Rohm, who have made such a staggering contribution.

In the months to come I hope to be allowed to produce two mighty tomes featuring creations of the two masters named above.

Fine folds are coming from Great Britain—watch for Eric Kenneway. From the Argentine we have the wonderful collection of folds by the late and much beloved Ligia Montoya; from Spain and the Latin countries emerges the name of Adolfo Cerceda; from Hong Kong, Philip Shen; from Switzerland, Dr. Emanuel Mooser; and from the birthplace of Origami, Japan, a very long list dominated by Akira Yoshizawa.

I must take this opportunity of thanking television viewers for their interest in my Origami programme, and it may be gratifying to know that the same series is being screened in Sweden.

So . . . spread the news about this delightful diversion, so inexpensive, so relaxing, and so challenging.

London   ROBERT HARBIN

INTRODUCTION

Origami stands poised midway between art and game. It is an art bound by strict and simple rules like those of a game; or it is a game that can produce a work of art. Origami resembles a chess problem on the one hand, and the act of musical composition on the other. Because it has rules, and because the field of action is limited from the start, Origami is an activity in which perfection is attainable.

The creation of a successful Origami figure requires, of course, an extraordinary ingenuity; any good model is a little marvel of engineering, a triumph of imagination over limitations. In the words of the sculptor and painter George Rhoads: 'The beauty of Origami is the beauty of economy. Everything is put to good use—no idle points are hidden away, there is no clumsy thickness, no complex device that could be simplified.' This beauty of economy—the perfect matching of means to ends—is the beauty of fine engineering, and it is hardly too much to say that Origami is a technological art form.

The ingenuity embodied in Origami explains, perhaps, the strength of its appeal to those who love cleverness for its own sake: not only engineers, but magicians, puzzle-solvers, computer programmers, mathematicians, readers of science fiction—all of whom delight in the elegant solution or the revelation of an unexpected consequence of an idea. And it is perhaps the combination of strict rules with hard thinking that accounts for the presence of theologians such as Robert Neale and Philip Shen and philosophers such as Miguel de Unamuno and Koshio Uchiyama among the creators of Origami models. The appeal of Origami, however, is universal. The elemental square becomes as if by magic a highly developed logical structure—an ornament, a toy, a piece of sculpture. Something is conjured up from nothing. Children, who know a good thing when they see it, are invariably fascinated by Origami, and the folding of a piece of paper has many times served as an ice-breaker among the most sophisticated adults.

I

It is easy to understand the steadily growing popularity of Origami. Folding is a challenging and enjoyable process in itself, and the finished product is attractive. No tools are needed, the materials cost little, and there is nothing to clean up.

Any beginner naturally supposes that there is a vast tradition in China and Japan, and that the East must be filled with creators of Origami figures. This is not the case. The tradition, though it stretches back for centuries, consists of a static repertory of a few dozen excellent figures (and others less distinguished); and though folding has its place in etiquette, it is considered to be an occupation suitable primarily for children. As Philip Shen remarks: 'Origami, like any other art, must be constantly renewed by creative experimentation—and the recent Western achievements may, in a sense, give paper-folding back to China.'

Yoshizawa and Uchiyama, working essentially in isolation, have, to be sure, done much to revitalise the Japanese tradition. But today the great majority of new figures—there are hundreds of them, with more being devised all the time—are the work of Western folders. It is an interesting situation: an Eastern discipline, somewhat neglected, has been transplanted to the West, where it has taken root and begun to flourish. During recent years, Western folders have set for themselves and then solved a long series of problems, each more difficult than the last. By undertaking to fold complex and seemingly impossible subjects, they have carried Origami to a new level of technical maturity; three-dimensional figures, for example, have become possible through the integration of pleating and box-folding with the technical devices of the Japanese tradition. Standards of style and form have risen steadily, and Origami is beginning to be recognised as a legitimate medium for sculpture: major exhibitions have been held in Seattle and London during the past few months. The line-and-arrow code and the vocabulary used in printed instructions are now well established, and Origami has appeared on television with some regularity in England, France, Sweden, Mexico, and the United States. The British Origami Society, founded by Sidney French, has provided the hobby with a firm organisational framework; the Society, which maintains an Origami library and publishes a journal, has an active and enthusiastic membership. In America there are two periodicals devoted to Origami: *The Origamian* is a quarterly containing news and essays along with instructions for models; *The Flapping Bird* is a monthly devoted exclusively to instructions.

Among the principal influences on the remarkable development of Origami in the West have been the books of Robert Harbin. *Paper Magic*, published in 1956, was the first book in English to attempt a general survey of Origami, the first written from an adult viewpoint for an adult audience, the first to present new creations. (It was also the first important book on Origami to come to my attention; I studied it very thoroughly indeed, and even today I keep a copy always at hand.) *Secrets of Origami*, which appeared in 1963, is a big book in every way, an anthology of old and new models so well planned and so comprehensive that it is universally regarded as a classic. The pocket-sized *Origami*, which followed in 1969, reflects in miniature the pattern of its predecessors—something new with something old—and it has reached a large public, thanks to the missionary work of Mr. Harbin's television broadcasts. It is a pleasure to introduce *New Adventures in Origami*. May it have many sequels!

SAMUEL RANDLETT

THE ESSENTIALS
OF ORIGAMI

You will be anxious to go ahead and start work on the models in this book. First, though, there is some helpful information to be considered, and the following essential instructions must be read carefully.

It is a fact that most beginners are not able to follow diagrams and instructions easily and successfully, however carefully they may have been planned. As a rule, Origami illustrators try to cram into each page as much information as possible. This practice is welcomed by the enthusiast and the expert, because it means that the book will be able to explain a large number of models. Unfortunately, though, a page filled with diagrams completely bewilders most beginners.

I have borne this in mind while preparing this book, and you will notice that the earlier pages have been designed with no more than two or three diagrams per page. All the diagrams are clearly drawn, and contain helpful instructions and symbols to give you all possible help, and to explain the mainly standard models which bring you in touch with most of the Basic Folds.

A Basic Fold is a fold from which many models can be made. There are many Basic Folds, both ancient and modern, and this book introduces you to some entirely new ones.

Always fold carefully, accurately, and neatly. If you fold carelessly, the result will be disastrous.

Study each diagram showing the complete folded model. Then, and only then, place your Origami paper in front of you and make your first fold.

When you make a fold, always crease the paper firmly with the back of your thumbnail. Good creases make folding easy, and are an invaluable guide later in the model, when you are making a series of folds.

Pre-creasing is an important feature. Consider, for example, Jack Skillman's Jackstone.

Notice how he pre-creases the paper he uses so that every-thing folds into place at the right moment.

Before you make a Reverse Fold, pre-crease the paper by folding the whole thickness before opening the paper and making the fold (see Reverse Folds).

Notice how paper coloured on one side is used to get the maximum effect for each model. The subject of paper is an important one. Origami paper (which is available from a variety of sources) should be strong, thin, and suitably coloured. But if you cannot lay hands on special Origami paper, almost any paper may be used.

If you are instructed to use a square of paper, make sure that it really is square, and that a rectangle is a true rectangle. Most of the models in this book are based on squares of paper, but there is no regular rule about this, as all shapes of paper can be used, according to the model's needs. See, for example, Ligia Montoya's Xmas Tree.

Origami is not meant to be a simple art. To the expert, it is a challenge to the eye, the brain, and the fingers, a wonderful mental and physical therapy.

When you fold one of the decorations explained in this book, you will find that by altering this or that fold you can invent endless shapes. In fact, you can doodle for hours.

When you have mastered the Basic Folds, you will then be equipped to produce figures and shapes of your own. Have something in mind, and then consider the best Base from which to start. See what you can do with the Neal Elias Figure Base, and Fred Rohm's Simplex Base.

Watch out for terms like Squash Fold. It is so named because you do just that—squash the part indicated so that the sides bulge and it flattens, in most cases symmetrically.

Study the Petal Folds, the Rabbit's Ears, and the various Bases, and try to remember what they are. If you get stuck, have a look at the Contents and refer to the page or pages concerned.

You will notice that certain procedures are used over and over again. You will soon get used to these and be able to carry them out automatically.

When you have folded everything in the first half of the book, you will find that more and more diagrams begin to appear on each page, and that the symbols begin to play a bigger part than the instructions. Many folds are included which have only symbols to guide you and so teach you to use them freely.

Start at the beginning of the book and work your way slowly and steadily through. Do not attempt anything too difficult to start with, because this can only end in disappointment.

If you are making a long train journey, take this book with you and fold a piece of paper to pass the time during your journey. Find a friend with the same interest, and you will both pass many a happy hour.

For the rehabilitation of damaged hands there is nothing like Origami for making reluctant fingers come back to life.

Finally—take it slowly; fold carefully, neatly, and accurately. And START AT THE BEGINNING.

SYMBOLS

The symbols used in this book are based on Akira Yoshizawa's code of lines and arrows. Symbols must become second nature to you when folding, but you will find that they are easy to acquire.

The moment you see a line of dashes, you know that the paper must be Valley Folded along that line. When you see a line of dashes and dots, you recognise the sign for a Mountain Fold. To make a Mountain Fold, you naturally turn the paper upside down and make a Valley Fold.

Arrows show the directions in which you must fold: left, right, up, down, in front, behind, and into.

You will notice one arrow which shows that a drawing has been enlarged for clarity. Another arrow indicates that a model must be opened out (see the Jackstone and others). My own special little black arrow indicates that you must sink, press, squeeze, or push in at certain points.

The symbols are in fact self-explanatory. They are simple common sense, and can be learnt in about ten minutes.

Try to use the symbols only and ignore explanations. This will help you when you come to read Japanese Origami books.

Study these symbols carefully

Valley fold

Mountain fold

Cut

Creases

X-Ray view

Hold here   ◯   Watch this spot   ✕

Fold in front

Fold behind

Push in, sink
or squash

Open out

Turn over

Fold over and over

Repeat a fold
shown here twice

8

Procedures Use of symbols

These symbols produce a waterbomb base

When creased

this fold results

When turned inside out these folds produce each other

When creased

this fold results

Known as a preliminary fold

Procedures   Squash Folds

Marked with symbols like

this   this   and this

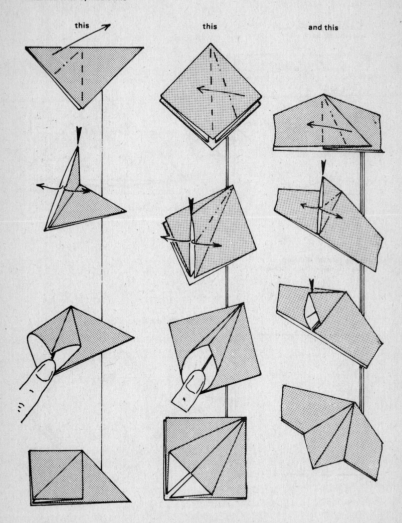

Procedures Petal Folds

Marked with symbols like

this   this   and this

Crease first   Crease first

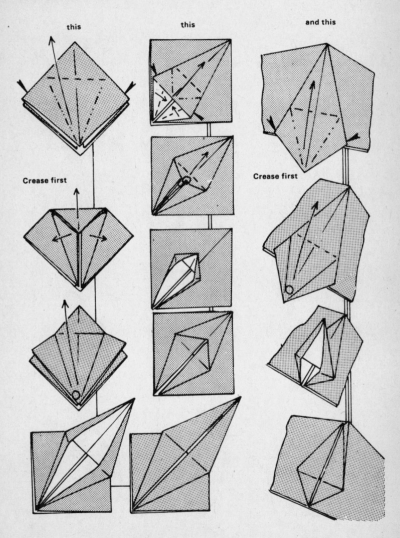

II

Procedures   Reverse Fold

Reverse fold or push in

Crease first

then reverse

These symbols ask for—

— this result

This is an outside reverse fold

A combination of the two

12

Procedures   Rabbit's Ears

This combination of symbols
denote a Rabbit's ear

Two other forms
of Rabbit's ears

First crease
this way

Then this
way

Then form
the ear

Procedures   Crimp   Single and Double

Crease
first
the
double
thickness

then fold so

Crease first the
double thickness

Then fold so

Crease first the
double thickness
then reverse fold
twice or push in

14

Procedures Sinking

This combination of symbols
means sink

First crease

This could also be a
reverse fold

Stretch the creased area

To form

this

or this

Picture Frame Florence Temko America

Use a colourful
paper square

Valley fold flaps

Fold 4 corners

Turn over

Like this

Picture Frame Put a picture in

Bring
ends
together

Tuck one end
into the other
and press flat

17

Dippy Dog   John Smith   England

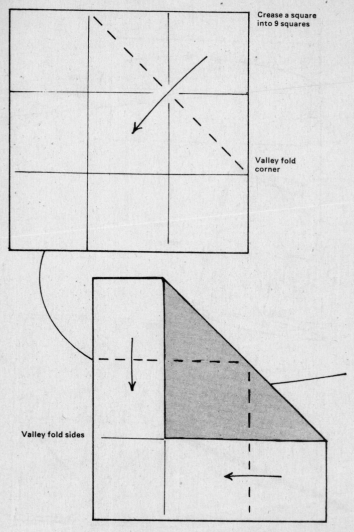

Crease a square into 9 squares

Valley fold corner

Valley fold sides

Dippy Dog   The Body

Mountain fold corner —

Then turn over —

Make a Rabbit's ear

Dippy Dog   Body continued

Mountain fold
narrow edges

Now mountain
fold in half

Rabbit's ear

Body now ready
for nodding head

Dippy Dog   The Head

Crease a square with
valley folds as shown

Turn over

Valley fold two corners
crease
then unfold

Turn over

2I

Dippy Dog   Head continued

Valley fold sides

Then the
top flap

Half done
now press flat

Mountain fold flap

22

Dippy Dog   Head continued

Valley
fold
flaps

Valley fold
flaps
then fold
in half

Hold as shown
pull nose down

Balance head
on body

23

Vase Folding without words

Vase   Symbols only

Vase   Note the Repeat signs

Vase   Crease 8 times

27

Vase   You struggle here

Vase   Well?

You can make the Vases
any size you wish
by widening the creases
which form the base

29

Party Hat   David Neale (age 10)   U.S.A.

Start with a
creased square

Just follow the symbols

open out the hat
and turn up the
corners indicated

Tree   Robert Harbin   England

Fold flaps
to diagonal
open out

Valley
fold
small
flaps

① ②

Then re-fold as   Turn over

③ ④ ⑤

A B

Fold flaps and
let A and B flip
to the front

Turn over

32

Tree continued

Fold as indicated

⑥
⑦
⑧
⑨

form trunk
of tree

⑩

33

Helmet   Ligia Montoya   Argentina

34

Helmet One of a large collection

Ocean Liner Peter Johnson (age 10) England

Crease square
Valley fold corner

Corner flips
to front

Fold point

36

Make valley
creases
fold in half —

So

Noshi Traditional Japanese

A simple Noshi which is a good luck item given with anything

Other Noshis can be very complicated

**Tuck a Noshi
under the ribbon
of a gift**

Noshi continued

A gold paper band slides around the middle

The centre strip of yellow cellophane is the Noshi
Should be thin dried meat

Box   Double strength

Use a square grease-proof if you wish to use it

Fold in half behind

Box continued

Make this special
fold twice

So

and so

42

Box continued

Hold the points
and pull the
box open

43

Decoration

Use a square
of colourful paper

44

Decoration continued

Valley fold

Valley fold

unfold

45

Decoration continued

Lift flap

Push flap
under flap—

46

Decoration continued

So —

now squash
fold all four corners

Several squares
fit together
to make patterns

47

2-4-86
bjl

Ball   Jack Skillman   U.S.A.

Begin with a square
corners folded
to the middle

Fold corners behind
Allow flaps to flip
outwards —

48

Ball   First published in The Flapping Bird

— So

Make two of
different colours

Put them together
alternate colours

49

Pinwheel   Philip Shen   Hong Kong

Valley fold diagonal creases
crease only
marked lines

So

Crease between arrows

Do this
3 more times

Pinwheel continued

Now crease the
marked lines

Like this

Crease between arrows

Do this 3 more times

Pinwheel continued

Now form the creased square into a pinwheel

So —

52

Pinwheel continued

—and so

Fixed to handle

Dropped from a
height it will
spiral down

Double Purse   Endla Saar   America

Crease heavily into thirds
Use striped wrapping paper

Use a
6 x 4
rectangle

54

Double Purse continued

Valley fold
heavily
into sixths

Valley fold
heavily the
seven diagonals

Force one whole
section into
the other

Form into a
tube and twist

Double Purse continued

The top section
almost flat
Now flatten
the base

57

Catch the Fly   Alice Gray   U.S.A.

Use a square

Crease one diagonal

Fold the other

Crease only

58

Catch the Fly continued

**Now fold flaps under
creases made
will work**

So

**Now open up
one side**

59

Catch the Fly continued

—and Valley fold the triangle as you fold side back into place

Repeat

Crimp neck

Fold wing flaps and —

60

Catch the Fly   Did you ?

— see how neck folds
   come into place

Witch   Robert Harbin   England

Mountain fold flaps

Valley fold flaps

Valley fold flaps

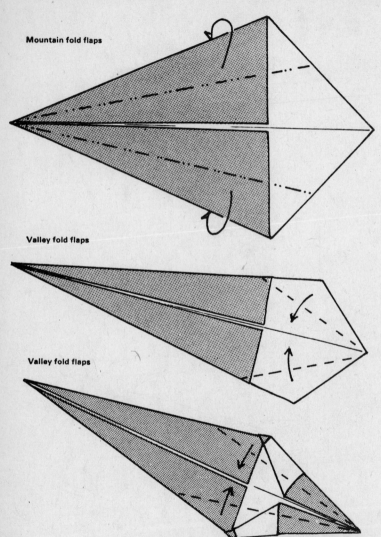

62

Witch   First published in the Flapping Bird

Fold in half

Reverse fold point

Reverse fold again

63

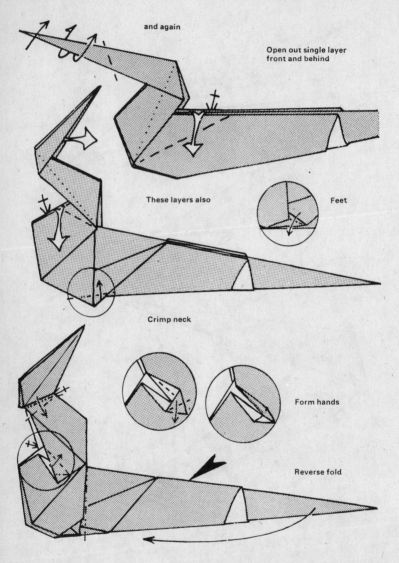

and again

Open out single layer
front and behind

These layers also

Feet

Crimp neck

Form hands

Reverse fold

64

Form hat

Reverse fold twice

Form broom

65

Tropical Bird   Ligia Montoya   Argentina

Fold flaps in

Ears half
done

and complete

Fold in half

Reverse fold

Make two
Rabbit's ears

66

Tropical Bird continued

Reverse fold

Form beak

Sink

Study the symbols

Xmas Tree   Ligia Montoya   Argentina

Use a square
Fold two sides to middle
and cut along creases

Make two Rabbit's ears
or Fish Base (page 72)

Xmas Tree   continued

Do not
press
ears flat

Fold long
flaps to
centre

Long flaps
behind
Flip to front —

— Fold short
flaps to
centre
and fold
point behind
at the
same time

69

Xmas Tree continued

Make 10
mountain folds

—Like this

Crimp
4 times

Crease as for
Water Bomb Base
and fold —

70

Xmas Tree   An immaculate fold

Press flat all small folds behind

— So

Angel Fish Robert Harbin England

1. Crease diagonals

2.

The fish base

3.

4. Fold point up

5.

6. Lift and squash

7. Turn over

B   A

72

Angel Fish continued

Lift B and squash

⑧

Petal fold B

⑨

⑩ Repeat fold A

Turn over

Fold Tail

⑪

Fold A and B

Frisbee Ed Sullivan U.S.A.

**You need 9
8 cm squares
of different
colours**

Make 8 Fish bases
(page 72)

Hold as indicated

Pull fins out

Points move in

Press flat

74

Frisbee   It sails thro' the air

Lock the 8 together

Ease the ninth
square inside

75

Dachshund   Paul Castles   England.

Make a Fish base
this way or
see page 72

Open out
single layer
under
point

76

Dachshund continued

Fold up

Turn over

Valley fold flaps
Watch X's
and squash flat

Turn over

77

Dachshund continued

Valley fold in half

Reverse fold head

Crimp head

Crimp tail

Reverse fold head

78

Hold as indicated
pull to sink head

Neolithic Man   Edward Megrath   England

Crease diagonals
Valley fold flap to
point indicated

V. fold to point indicated

Hold and pull point down

80

Reverse fold nose
in and out

Flaps raised to
show folds

Fold flaps to
complete nose

Fold top lip in

Make the mouth work

Crease then
reverse fold
bottom lip

Seated Cat   Pat Crawford U.S.A.

Begin with Fish base
(page 72)

Fold in half
squash and
petal fold feet

Two reverse folds

83

Seated Cat continued

So

**Bring white surface
to the front - turn
inside out**

So

**Move chest
over left
Fold head down**

Reverse fold

**Open out head
and fold up**

Crimp tail

Seated Cat continued

Like this

Now complete head
and paws

85

Bird Base   A Basic fold

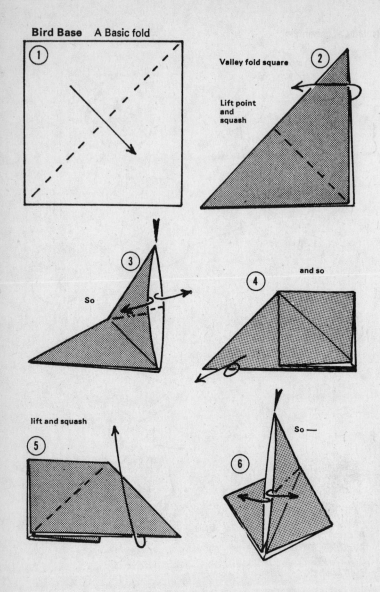

①

② Valley fold square

Lift point
and
squash

③ So

④ and so

⑤ lift and squash

⑥ So —

Bird Base and Preliminary Base

Preliminary base

⑦

— and so

⑧ Crease only

Crease flaps
and petal fold
both sides

⑨

⑩

⑪

⑫

Bird Base

87

Crane   Traditional Japanese

**Begin with a
Bird base**
(page 86)

Reverse fold points

Hold wings and pull

Crane   Good Luck Symbol

Stretched Bird Base

Begin with the
Bird Base (page 86)

This way up

Hold points and stretch

With fingers and thumbs
fold in half ——

Stretched Bird Base continued

— So

Now bring the points together
by moving fingers and thumbs
inwards —

So

The Stretched Bird Base

White Walrus   Robert Harbin   England

Start with a
Stretched Bird Base
page 90

Reverse fold
head

Reverse fold
tail

2 Rabbit's
ears
fold into
chest

92

Wedding Bells Mick Guy England

Start with the Stretched Bird Base
(page 90) and a metallic paper square

Form Rabbit's
Ears

Lay flat

Valley fold model

93

Wedding Bells continued

Crimp centre piece

Mountain fold flap

Valley fold flap

Turn over

94

Crimp tops

Petal fold
clappers

Make Double Valley
fold

95

Begin with Stretched Bird Base
(page 90)

Reverse fold points

Make colour-
change by
turning inside out

So—

Boy on a Dolphin continued

— and so

Mountain fold
long flaps

fold up both sides

Reverse fold

Crimp boy

Ease out extra paper

97

Form kneeling
posture

Crimp head

Extra paper

Crimp stomach

Mountain fold
snout

98

Boy on a Dolphin   continued

Complete head

Make Dolphin smile

99

Robin Joan Homewood England

Sink point

Begin with
the Bird Base
(page 86)

Colour
change
see page 96

Fold flap
to left

Now fold
2 flaps right

Again turn
white side out

Fold flap
left

Only crease
the point

Fold small
flaps behind

Robin continued

Fold out single layers bring X down

Fold head flap inside out —

Turn over

— so

102

Robin continued

Fold flaps
into pockets

Valley fold legs
3 times

Reverse fold legs

103

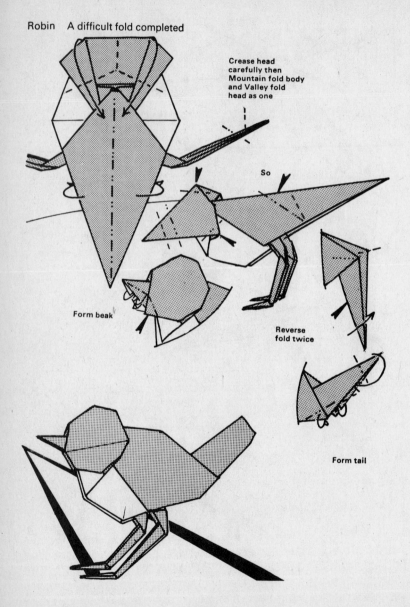

Robin   A difficult fold completed

Crease head
carefully then
Mountain fold body
and Valley fold
head as one

So

Form beak

Reverse
fold twice

Form tail

104

Super Star

Begin with the Bird Base

Fold flaps front and behind

Open out

Put thumbs inside and grip as shown

Watch the repeat arrows

Dagger   Colin Rowe (age 14)   England

Begin with Bird Base
(page 100)

Make a
Rabbit's Ear

and again

So

Fold flaps flat

Fold 4 flaps

Dagger   A fine bookmarker this

Reverse fold points
into Hilt

Fold 4 flaps

Double Dutch   Noel Stanton   England

Begin with the
preliminary base
(page 87)
Squash fold 4 flaps

Fold flap right
and pull out
'Tent' as marked

Double Dutch continued

Another tent fold

So

Fold to open

Fold single flaps
in front and behind

109

Double Dutch continued

Make Rabbit's Ear
and fold flap

Fold double flap

Petal fold

Fold long flap
and then point

So —

Double Dutch   Careful with the heads

Woman   Man

Crimp necks

Colour change
(page 96)

Rabbit's ear

Fold Bonnet
in

Flatten Umbrella
with fingers
and tweezers

Fold long
flap twice

III

Clerical Hat   Ligia Montoya   Argentina

Crease square and fold corners to the centre

Turn over

Crease and fold Water bomb base

Push in 4 corners single layer in front

So

Fold flaps behind

Super Salt Cellar   Philip Shen   Hong Kong

Crease diagonals
and fold 4 corners
to the centre

Crease only

114

Squash fold 4 points
of Water Bomb Base

Now
rotate
model

Petal fold the
four flaps

115

Or with fingers
and thumbs
pull out flaps
to make
Salt Cellar

Pull out
points
below
to form
dish
above

Moth   Tim Ward   England

Begin with the
Water Bomb Base
(page 113)

Fold antenae
under narrow body

119

Shapes and the Windmill Base

1. Crease a square and fold flaps

2. Fold again

3. Crease diagonals

4. Pull out two points

5. Like this

Now pull out the other two —

The Windmill Base continued

— Like this

Squash fold
all four points

See left

Now begin
the first design
make eight
Valley folds

Shapes   This is Doodling

Squash fold 8 corners

Mountain and Valley
fold corners
and points

Stop here if you wish

You could stop here
but go ahead and
fold corners

Fold 4 corners to
make feet

Shapes   Most of them make boxes

Insert left thumb and squeeze
together all 4 corners

So

Persian Helmet   Ligia Montoya   Argentina

Begin with a preliminary base (page 87)

Turn over

fold flaps
inside hat

Jackstone   Jack Skillman   U.S.A.

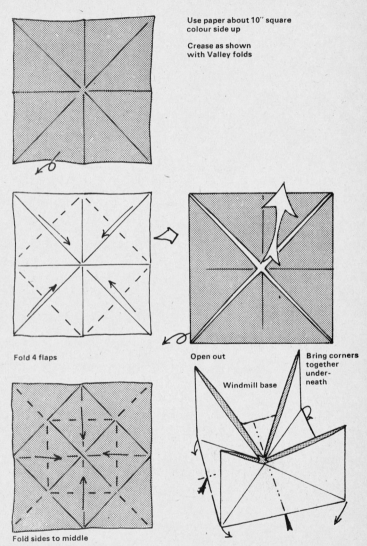

Use paper about 10″ square
colour side up

Crease as shown
with Valley folds

Fold 4 flaps

Open out

Windmill base

Bring corners
together
under-
neath

Fold sides to middle

125

Jackstone   First published in the Origamian

Press flat

Raise X and squash 4 times

Petal fold 4 times

So

Crease flap both ways

and so

Now open out flat

Jackstone   Pre-creasing

When opened out leave in creases

Now carefully Mountain and Valley fold
as indicated

Corner by corner press together (Mountain fold)
at the points shown

Careful manipulation will make model
take shape

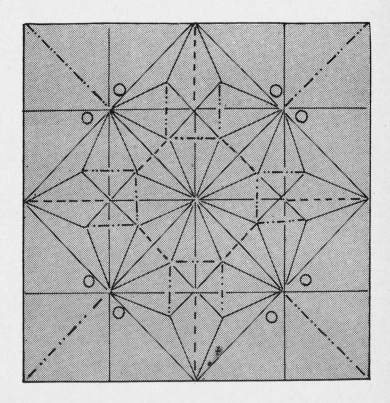

Here you see two corners in action
and the diamond shapes forming

Move to the other two corners
and persevere—

Jackstone   Struggle on

— until this shape
begins to appear

Keep pressing
together to get
this shape

Turn over and pre-fold
the four surfaces
shown

so

and so

129

Jackstone   Very difficult now

When 4 surfaces have
been creased turn over

Open out ringed area

Push surfaces
in either side
of centre

When complete
squash fold
the large flaps

130

Jackstone   Easier now

Like this

Mountain fold both flaps

The other similar
surfaces treated in
the same way

2 complete

All 8 flaps folded
Fold this flap over
to the left ——

Put 8 flaps into 4 pockets

Crease then fold
left and right flaps
into pocket

All
flaps
in
pockets

Now ease and pull out the 4 points
Middle becomes 3D
Now hold the middle and 3D the other
4 points —

Jackstone   You deserve a medal

— Like this

133

Basket   Japanese   Donated by Lillian Oppenheimer

Cut ⅓ off a square

134

Basket continued

quite difficult

Knight in Armour   Neal Elias   U.S.A.

Large silver
foil square

Crease and
fold flaps

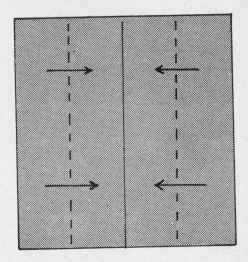

Complete folds and crease corners

Elias special base for figures

Sink the creased corners

So

The Base completed grip the points below ——

Hold and pull all 4 corners to the middle by stretching

Top view

138

Knight in Armour   This just happens

— and stretch

Stretch and move fingers and thumbs
inwards as shown

Finally flatten

Now Valley fold
long flap

Knight in Armour   Don't be afraid of this

Hold legs and fold inwards
open body and fold skirt
behind legs

Front

Back

Knight in Armour   Crucial folds

Crimp the body

So

Fold arms down

Fold body flaps first then skirt flaps

Crimp the shoulder piece

Knight in Armour   Special care

Make special crimps to form arms

So

Crimp Gauntlets

Form leg and foot armour

Fold flaps to form shoulders and helmet

Knight in Armour   Magnificent !

143

Skier   Robert Harbin   England

Begin with Elias figure
base (page 138)

Mountain fold
long flaps
forming arms
at the same time

Pull skis down

So

Form legs below
the knee
and fold feet
to skis

Knee fold, tips
body back

144

Skier continued

Like this

Reverse fold body

Valley fold skis

Reverse fold
head section

Narrow arms
fold posterior

Colour change skis
(page 96)

Skier continued

Form the woollen cap

Make small fold for face

Super Hat Ligia Montoya Argentina

Begin with the Water Bomb Base
(page 113)

Valley fold

Sink

Fold both flaps

Fold the long flap
left repeat

Reverse fold edge

Flower and Leaf   Toshie Takahama   Tokyo

Begin with Frog Base
(page 151)

This way
up

Open out
flower

Move top
flap left

So

Fold point
down

Move and refold
single layer

Then fold point up

Flower and Leaf continued

So

Make the leaf
out of a
square green
all over

Shh! just a little glue

149

Plumed Helmet Ligia Montoya Argentina

Begin with the Water Bomb Base
(page 113)

I50

Old Kentucky Horse Raymond K. M'Lain U.S.A.

Begin with the preliminary base
(page 87)

Squash fold 4 corners

Petal fold
4 flaps

The Frog base

Fold 4 flaps
down

So

Tuck triangle
inside front
and back

So

Hold points
indicated and
pull to do this

Now open out
completely and
turn upside down

Pinch
together
at points
indicated
and push
together —

Old Kentucky Horse continued

— So

Form Rabbit's ears
and move them up

Now repeat behind

153

Now pull open as shown

and rotate to this position

Crease corners
Push sides in ⟶

— Like this

Fold two legs up

X   **X**

Open up the front —

155

So

Bring the bottom triangle
up into the open section

The top triangle
swings down

Cover up the
triangle ——

156

—Like this

Fold model in half

Lift the legs up and
let the nose move down

Nose down

Tuck X on both sides into
the pocket behind

Legs folded down and
X tucked behind

Now squash fold legs ——

158

Old Kentucky Horse continued

— Like this

Petal fold all 4 legs

Valley fold 4 legs

Old Kentucky Horse continued

Fold head flap under when eased from behind leg

Below turn inside out
(colour change page 96)

Both hind legs X

This flap also – then fold leg right

Like this

Reverse fold both points

Fold flaps into body

Open legs below and
lift flap upwards

Reverse fold legs

Fold flap
into
body

Repeat behind

Fold flaps into head

Reverse fold tail and legs

Fold half leg into other half

Form tail

Crimp neck

Crimp legs

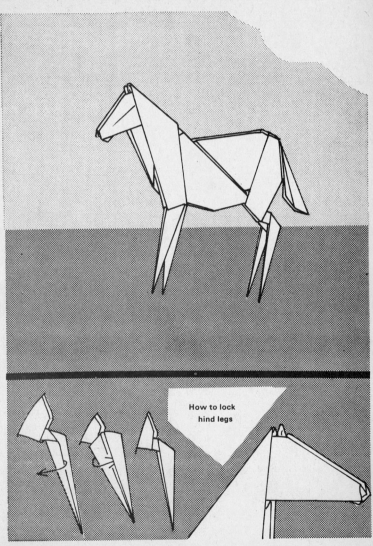

How to lock
hind legs

Kangaroo   E. G. Langridle   England

**Use thin strong
brown paper
30 cms square**

Crease as shown

Start folding

A Rabbit's Ear

Rabbit's ear squashed

Make the preliminary base
(page 87)

Fold in all corners
to make a Bird Base
(page 86)

Hold the two points for—

Kangaroo continued

a Stretched Bird Base
(page 90)

Now bring the two
points together

Make a Rabbit's Ear
of X

Turn over

Petal fold

X Rabbit's Ear

Watch the reverse
folds carefully

Finishing touches
Look for every symbol

Kangaroo   traced from the original

Medieval Hat   Robert Harbin   England

Use 3 x 2 rectangle

Tuck in

Like this

172

Simplex Base Fred Rhom U.S.A.

With this unique base
Fred Rhom has produced
many masterpieces

Simplex base

173

Snake Charmer   Fred Rohm   U.S.A.

Begin with the Simplex Base
(page 173)

Begin with colour side up
Use metallic foil

Colour change
(page 96)

Crimp neck

Push up
centre
open out

Colour
change

Inside
view

So

Sink into
head

Press flat

Move X up
in a crimp
both sides

Flute complete

175

Snake Charmer continued

Inside view
of arm folds

Sink

Snake Charmer continued

Crease only

60°

Colour change
(page 96)

Crease then fold

Three reverse folds for snake

Hat and Fox Puppet Japanese

Crease a square and fold in half
Squash fold flaps

So

Fold up corners
(repeat behind)

Fold twice

Otomo Nu Koronushi   From the Kan No Mado

A white square traditionally
precoloured
Cut as shown
Make poet and colour
afterwards

Otomo Nu Koronushi Folded from ancient drawings by Sydney French   England

Crease carefully
and fold a
Preliminary Base

Crease and
push
in four
flaps

Pull out
extra
paper

181

Lift flap over the
top put head through

Reverse fold

Otomo No Koronushi continued

Crease and push in shoulders

Make tiny gold paper ring
for top notch

183

Otomo Nu Koronushi   One of Six Poets